The Magick

Attract the Work You Love
with Angelic Power

Damon Brand

THE GALLERY OF
MAGICK

CONTENTS

Finding a Job   7

The Steps to Success   9

The Magickal Mindset   11

To Discover New Jobs and Make Your Talents Known   15

To Increase Your Appeal to Employers   17

To Win a Job   19

On The Day of Your Interview   21

To Increase Your Chance of Success   23

Letting Go of Results   25

When the Magick Works   27

Finding a Job

This book can work for you whether you are unemployed, seeking a promotion or looking for a completely new job that's better than your old job.

Magick can make the difference between getting what you want, and the all-too-familiar struggle.

As soon as *Magickal Cashbook* was published, I discovered that lots of people wanted more than a quick bag of cash. It's great to get an unexpected rush of money, but for so many people, a regular job that pays well counts more in the long run. With the help of my group, The Gallery of Magick, I've been working on books that cover various aspects of success, including career and wealth building, but I've found out that for so many people, the urgent need in the modern world is much simpler. They just want a new job.

The solution is a book that shows you how to use magick to get a job. This book is aimed at the unemployed, and those seeking a change of employment.

We could give this book away for free, but have found that magick works best when there is some sort of trade, deal or pact in place. We've made it as low-cost as possible, because it is clear that some people will not be able to afford much more.

One of the difficulties I find when writing books of this kind is that they are meant to be useful to experienced occultists, but they are designed for beginners too. I know that many beginners will not be familiar with banishing, will fall asleep at the mention of correspondences or planetary hours, and would rather I gave them a simple spell than a complex ritual. As such, the magick has to be simplified to the point where it will work safely, whatever your level of experience.

Magick cannot be made too simple, but nor should it be inaccessible. What we've developed here is the best magickal approach I know for securing a job.

I can't create more jobs and I can't change the economy, but I want to put a powerful magickal system in your hands.

A job can be worth millions of dollars to you over the years, so this should be an investment that pays off.

The Steps to Success

With magick, it is important to work in small steps. This is one of the greatest secrets of magick. If you have a goal, do not perform magick for that final goal. Instead, break it down into many smaller goals.

If you want to be a world-class soccer player, start with rituals that get you accepted into a good local team. Work on rituals that improve your skills. Use magick to make yourself appealing to teams and managers. And in this way, you gradually build up to your dream.

When it comes to job-seeking magick, this means that you shouldn't aim for impossible-to-achieve careers. Aim for something that seems just out of reach to you at the moment rather than something that seems absurd. If you aim for something that is just out of reach, you can get there.

I am not suggesting that you limit your dreams. You should dream big, but I know that people often hope magick will make everything change in an instant. Magick works by shifting the odds and ordering coincidences in your favor. It can change your life, but don't expect to be offered the top job at a company you've never worked at before. Break your dream down into stages and you will get there faster than you ever thought possible.

It's only fair to warn you that magick is just one factor in any given situation, and there are many other forces at work, and much competition. But magick is a powerful factor. It will make it easier for you to find work, prepare well, appeal to employers, impress them at interview and work on their minds while they sleep. In short, it can get you the job.

At the same time, you must do all the hard work you can in the real world. If you perform this magick and wait for somebody to employ you, or hope a promotion will appear on your desk, you're wasting your time.

Magick works best when you put in as much effort as you're asking these angelic forces to put into the working. That means you must look for work, prepare properly for the interview, dress well and genuinely work to be the best person for the job. If you do that, magick will take your efforts a long, long way.

The magickal seals in this book have been created by combining ancient secrets with modern magickal technology and give you near-instant access to angelic and spiritual powers.

This book is much shorter than other books by The Gallery of Magick, so that it can be made available cheaply, and used rapidly. If you have concerns about the safety of the magick, or questions about why it works, please read my other books, or look at the FAQs on this website:

www.galleryofmagick.com

The Magickal Mindset

It's important to get into a slightly altered state of consciousness before each ritual.

Sit in a quiet place where you won't be disturbed and say the words NAH-KAH EE-AH-OH-EH over and over until you feel a sense of calm come over you. If you feel nothing, don't worry, just stay relaxed and move onto the next step. (The words are a way of saying you wish to recognize divine power, and this statement has a strong effect on your ability to work magick.)

Imagine the sun. Imagine it as a vast ball of heat and flame, and then see it shrinking. As the sun shrinks, it moves inside your heart and resides there as a star. Imagine this tiny pinprick of light within your heart, containing all the massive power and heat of the sun.

Don't worry if your imagination is not perfectly clear. All you need to do is imagine that the sun has shrunk and is now a tiny star in your heart.

You are now prepared to perform any of the following rituals. Do not worry about getting everything right, or pronouncing everything perfectly. This is a robust system that responds to your desire. Where non-English languages are used, I put the phonetic pronunciation in BLOCK CAPITALS.

Some of the pronunciations may seem strange at first. The angelic name Poiel, for example, is pronounced PAW-EE-ELL. PAW sounds like a cat's *paw*. EE sounds like *bee* without the *b*. ELL sounds like *bell* without the *b*. It's not the pronunciation you might expect for the name Poiel, but it works.

The books are Pronunciation Proof, because of the visual sigils, so you don't need to stress about getting it right.

Be aware that these words and names can be pronounced in many ways, but what's shown here is a good compromise between ease of use and accuracy. What you say will work just fine.

If you want more guidance, The Gallery of Magick website contains a video tutorial on pronunciation. I believe, however, that if you read what you see here, it will work.

Be assured that when you call the spirits, using their name and sigil, they can hear you. You don't even need to print the sigils or copy them from this book. Looking at the page is enough for it to work, even if you're using the ebook.

When the ritual is finished close this book and go about your day as you normally would. If you keep thinking about the magick, distract yourself by eating, running or doing some other physical activity.

It is vital that you don't lust for results. You have handed your request over to the spirits, so do not hassle and annoy them by worrying and pondering and checking up on them. Don't keep checking your voicemail or email to see if the job offer is in. That will make you seem insecure.

At the same time, you must put in all the effort you can in the real world. The spirits will meet you half way. Look for suitable jobs all the time, prepare well, perform at your best and you will get what you seek.

Perform no more than one ritual a day, unless you have to (because an interview comes up suddenly, for example.) You can perform each ritual once, or keep repeating it as you go about your job hunting. There is no set rule or obligation, so just perform the rituals when it feels like your job-seeking needs a boost.

To Discover New Jobs and Make Your Talents Known

Invoke the power of Aniel.

Gaze at the sigil for a few moments and consider that you will soon find jobs that appeal to you, and that make the most of your talents. Know that the power of Aniel will make you appear wiser than others around you.

Then say:

EEM AH-MAHR-TEE
MAH-TAH RAH-GUH-LEE
HAHS-DUH-KAH
EE-AH-OH-EH
YEES-AH-DAY-NEE

Speak to Aniel, saying, 'Oh great spirit Aniel (AH-KNEE-ELL), reveal to me the work that I love to do, guide me to use my talents and let me appear wise to those who would employ me.'

Chant the word ABB-DAH, while looking at this sigil for at least two minutes. Allow yourself to feel grateful that you found the work you wanted (*as though* it has already happened).

To Increase Your Appeal to Employers

Invoke the power of Vehuel.

Gaze at the sigil for a few moments and consider that all who meet you will admire you. Know that the power of Vehuel will make your talents and virtues known so that you stand out from the crowd.

Then say:

**GAH-DOWL EE-AH-OH-EH
OO-MEH-HOO-LAHL
MEH-AWED
VEH-LEE-GUH-DOO-LAH-TOE
AIN HI-KERR**

Speak to Vehuel, saying, 'Oh great spirit Vehuel (VAY-WHO-ELL), make my talents known, and make my personality shine so that all who meet me are drawn to work with me.'

Chant the word MAH-RAH, while looking at this sigil for at least two minutes. Think of nothing other than the sound you are making. If you find yourself thinking about the job you want, simply be grateful that you got the job (as *though* it has already happened).

To Win a Job

Invoke the power of Poiel.

Gaze at the sigil for a few moments and consider that your talent and personality will win you the job you seek. Know that in any interview situation you will be well-liked.

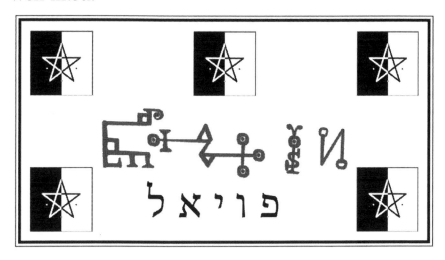

Then say:

KEY RAW-TSAY
EE-AH-OH-EH
BEH-AH-MAW
YEH-FAH-AIR
AH-NAH-VEEM
BEE-SHOO-AH

Speak to Poiel, saying, 'Oh great spirit Poiel (PAW-EE-ELL), give me esteem and fortune to obtain the job I desire.'

Chant the word ILL-EE, while looking at this sigil for at least two minutes. Think of nothing other than the sound you are making, and enjoy the feeling of having been given the job you want (*as though* it has already happened.) If you are seeking several jobs, enjoy the feeling of having been given a job you love, without being too specific.

On The Day of Your Interview

On the day of your interview invoke the power of Torquaret. No sigil is required for this ritual.

Torquaret will make you seem appealing and persuasive to your audience. You will appear to be performing well and answering the questions correctly during your interview.

In a quiet space, sit or stand facing East, and repeat the phrase:

NAH-KAH EE-AH-OH-EH

Repeat this phrase until you feel that you are beginning to relax and that your mind is entering a trance-like state. You don't need to be out of your mind; just let yourself relax into a magickal state of mind as you say these words. When you feel ready, call on the angel Raziel (who can be called by using the name Arzel) by saying the following three times:

KOH-SUE HAH-REE-EEM TZIL-AH
VAH-ANNA-FEHA ARE-ZELL

You may feel a presence on the first call. You may sense a bright white light, or smell the scent of trees, or hear pleasant, calming noises. If you don't feel much, or anything, don't worry - Raziel is listening. Raziel comes when called and helps to empower the rest of the ritual.

Now say, 'I call on Raziel (RAH-ZEE-ELL) to connect me to the power of magick. Mighty Torquaret (TORE-KOO-ARE-ET), know that I command thee to give me the power to persuade and enchant those who interview me. Impress those that I speak to at all times. I command you with the word of power AH-RAH-REE-TAH.'

Feel a brief *thank You*, directed towards the angel Torquaret, and to the spirit of Raziel who has overseen the operation.

These spirits are powerful, but they came because you called, and because it is their duty to serve those who call them. Do not beg, worship or pray to them. Thank them politely, and know that they are dismissed, ready to do the work as they have been instructed.

To Increase Your Chance of Success

When you return home from any job interview, invoke the power of Farris to make your work more likely to succeed. Ideally, you should perform this ritual about an hour after sunset.

Gaze at the sigil for a few moments and consider that your success is assured, and that any job you could benefit from can be yours.

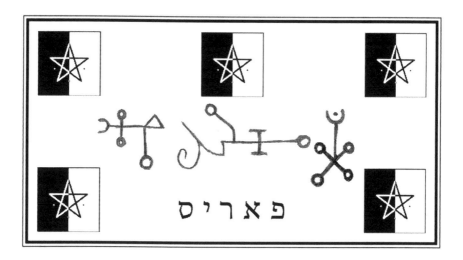

Then say:

TAW-DEE-AIN-EE
OR-RAHK HAY-EEM
SOW-VAH SEM-A-HAWT
ET-PAH-NAY-KAH
NAY-EE-MOT BEE-ME-NAY-KAH
NET-SAHK

Speak to Farris, saying, 'Oh great spirit Farris (FAR-REES), ensure the success of my work.' Speak with sincerity and repeat this three times.

The process that follows is a little different to the rituals that have gone before. Continue to gaze at the sigil and know that Farris is listening, but ask yourself the following questions. After you ask each question, just ponder for a moment, as though you actually have the job, and wonder how it all went so well. Do not actually try to answer the questions.

These are the questions you should ponder:

Why did I prepare so well for this job?

Why are my talents so perfect for this job?

Why was it so easy for me to get the job I wanted?

Why did they love me at the interview?

Why did they offer me the job?

After a moment, thank Farris silently, put the book aside and do something that distracts you from thoughts about your job.

Letting Go of Results

When you perform a ritual, you are asking for another power to do some of the work for you. You are handing the task over to various spirits and powers. Trust that these forces will go to work for you. The best way to show your trust is to forget about your magick.

Keep working at job seeking, but don't worry about whether you'll get a particular job. Just assume it's all under control and it's only a matter of time until everything comes together the way you want. This gives you enormous power.

The spirits will do what you ask, so show your trust by letting go of your lust for result. Feel grateful that the result will come about.

This can be a tricky mental balancing act, but it is the one you must master for magick to work. If you have difficulty with this, remember the questions that came after you summoned Farris. Go to a quiet place, and rather than worrying about what job you might get, sit there and imagine you've got the job.

When we actually get something we really want, we often ponder how we got there, without seeking a genuine answer. When I earned my pilot's license, I spent several days saying to myself, 'How on earth did I manage that? Why was I able to learn to do such good landings?' And yet I was never really looking for an answer. The act of asking is an acknowledgment that a dream has come true.

So, if you find yourself worrying, just sit and pretend you already have the job and ask yourself,

'How did I manage that?' and lots of other similar questions, just as though it's already happened. You'll find this generates lots of pleasant feelings and is better than worrying about magickal results.

The sooner you stop worrying and waiting, the faster the results come. This trust in magick can take time to develop, but it is the best way to get results fast. Act as though the results don't really matter - as though something will come along sooner or later - and you set extremely powerful wheels in motion.

When the Magick Works

Be careful what you wish for. Magick works, and if you perform a ritual to get a job you don't really want, you may be stuck with that job for a while. Of course, you can use the magick all over again to change jobs, but try to be wise from the outset.

If you are desperate to get employment, then of course any job will do, but even then, try to find something that appeals to you, so that you're not merely a wage slave.

If you want a quick burst of cash then have a look at *Magickal Cashbook*, which costs just a few dollars and could get you enough money for new clothes for your interview.

The magick in this book works easily for most people, but if you find it difficult, *The Gallery of Magick* website contains many FAQs, along with advice and practical information that is updated on a regular basis.

If you have questions, our website is an excellent source of background material and practical posts that help you to get magick working. We could have published two or three books on magickal practice, but instead, it's all there for free. I urge you to make good use of the site, when you encounter problems, and also when you wish to expand your understanding of magick. There are new posts every few weeks, and they can help keep your magick vital and hone your understanding.

If you are curious about the source of this magick, I can say that modern magick is based on recent discoveries, private collections and entire libraries of documents and texts. Providing a bibliography for this book would be almost impossible, but if you are fascinated by the theory, there is some background information on the website. You will also learn more by exploring practical magick.

If you have an interest in developing your practical magick further, there are many texts that can assist you and you'll find out about them on the website.

Damon Brand

www.galleryofmagick.com

Made in the USA
Monee, IL
25 March 2021